SHAPES

Carol Watson

Illustrated by David Higham

Consultant: Wyn Brooks

Deputy-Head Teacher of The Coombes School,
Arborfield, Berkshire; lectures widely on
Primary School Mathematics.

There are shapes all around us.

Look at this shape.

It is a town.
It is made up of different shapes.

3

People have shapes.

Animals have shapes.

Can you match up the shapes?

Some shapes have straight lines.

This is a straight line.

Other shapes have curved lines.

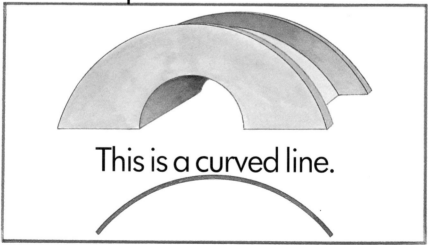

This is a curved line.

Which shapes have straight lines?
Which have curved lines?
Which have both?

Some shapes fit together easily.

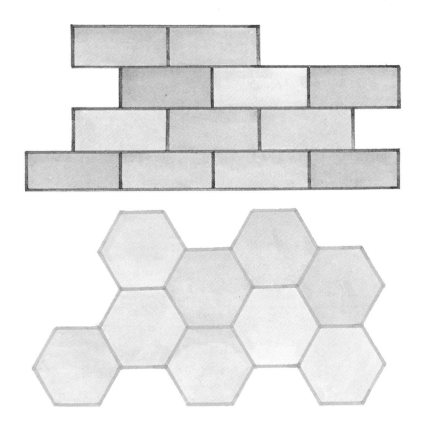

When shapes fit together
without gaps it is called tessellation.

Some shapes leave spaces even when they are put close together.

They do not tessellate because they have curved edges.

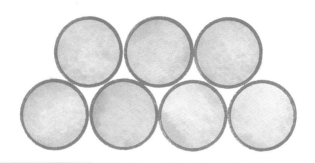

Which of these shapes do you think will tessellate?

When two lines meet they make a corner.

This is
a corner →

This is
a corner →

Look at all these shapes.
Which of them have corners?

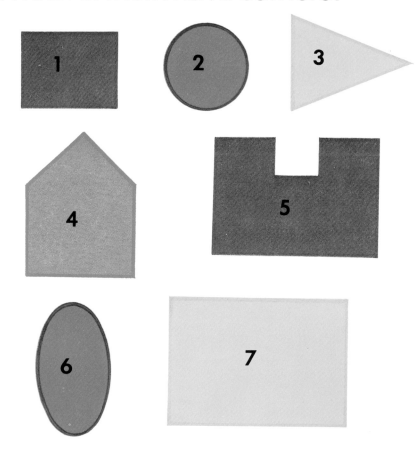

How many corners can you find?

Ben is building a garage.

His wood is different shapes.

This is a square shape.

How many edges
has it got?

How many corners
are there?

This shape is a rectangle.

How many
edges and
corners
are there?

What is the difference between
a square and a rectangle?

Look at Ben's house and garage.

How many squares can you find?

How many rectangles can you find?

The children are sailing their boat
in the park.

Each sail has a shape.
It is called a triangle.

Here are some triangles.

Each one has
three edges
and three corners.

Puzzle Picture.

How many triangles can you see
in the picture?

Ben waves to Rose. She rides her bicycle.

The bicycle wheels are round.

A round shape is called a circle.

It has a
curved
edge.

Does it have any corners?

How many more circles can
you find in the picture?

Which is the odd one out in each of these groups?

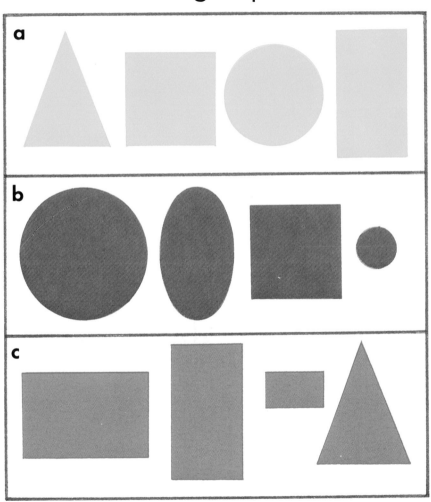

Ben has put tiles on the wall but he has left one out.

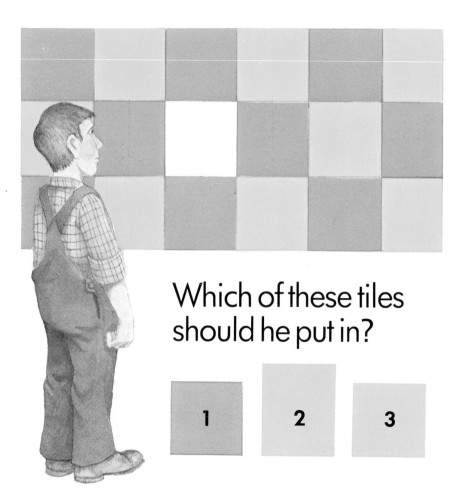

Which of these tiles should he put in?

1   2   3

The circus has come to town.

How many different shapes can

you find?

Answers

Page 7
straight lines – star, pencil
curved lines – moon.
curved and straight lines – bottle,
car, bucket, cup, spade, spoon.

Page 9
Square and diamond will tessellate

Page 11
No. 1 – four corners
No. 3 – three corners
No. 4 – five corners
No. 5 – eight corners
No. 7 – four corners
24 corners altogether

Page 13
square – four edges and four corners
rectangle – four edges and four corners

A square has 4 edges of equal length.
A rectangle has 4 edges, but each pair
of edges is of equal length.

Page 14
14 squares
13 rectangles

Page 17
5 triangles

Page 19
A circle has no corners.
13 circles.

Page 20
a) circle
b) square
c) triangle

page 21
Tile no. 3

Page 22/23
16 squares on clown's trousers.
2 circles for clown's buttons.
2 circles for clowns' noses.
2 triangles for clown's bow tie.
2 circles – hoop
4 circles – plates being juggled by
clown
3 squares – buttons on clown's shirt
1 triangle – flag held by girl on horse
5 circles – monocycle
8 triangles – flags over road

Total – 19 squares
15 circles
11 triangles

First published 1983
Usborne Publishing Ltd
83-85 Saffron Hill
EC1N London, England
© Usborne Publishing Ltd 1983

The name of Usborne and the
device ☺ are Trade Marks of
Usborne Publishing Ltd.
Printed in Belgium by Casterman S.A.